THE BLITZ

Peter Doyle

SHIRE PUBLICATIONS

Published in Great Britain in 2014 by Shire Publications Ltd,
PO Box 883, Oxford OX1 9PL, United Kingdom.
PO Box 3985, New York, NY 10185-3983, USA.
E-mail: shire@shirebooks.co.uk   www.shirebooks.co.uk

A CIP catalogue record for this book is available from the
British Library.

Shire Library no. 606.   ISBN-13: 978 0 74780 804 6

Peter Doyle has asserted his right under the Copyright,
Designs and Patents Act, 1988, to be identified as the
author of this book.

Designed by Tony Truscott Designs, Sussex, UK
Typeset in Perpetua and Gill Sans.
Printed in China through World Print Ltd.

14 15 16 17 18   11 10 9 8 7 6 5 4 3 2

COVER IMAGE
Cover design and photography by Peter Ashley. Back cover
detail: ARP Warden badge, collection of Peter Ashley.

TITLE PAGE IMAGE
Coventry and its wrecked Owen Owen store after the raid
on 14 November 1940. (IWM H 5600)

CONTENTS PAGE IMAGE
A London shelter sign and Blackout paraphernalia.

DEDICATION
For Buster.

ACKNOWLEDGEMENTS
I am grateful to many friends who have discussed the Blitz
and its meaning with me. The many stories of personal
experience I have been granted through discussion with
people who lived through the bombardment of Britain's
cities have enriched my knowledge. Like many authors,
I am indebted to those whose written accounts have
similarly broadened my experience. Many of the personal
experiences recounted here are derived, with kind
permission of the BBC, from The People's War
(www.bbc.co.uk/ww2peopleswar), an archive built
between June 2003 and January 2006 that resulted in
47,000 personal stories and 15,000 images. Though
collected very much after the fact, this web archive
represents an extremely valuable resource for social
historians. I am grateful to Vicky Mitchell at the BBC for
facilitating my use of this. Many others provided help and
advice: Bella Bennett, Paul Evans and Dr Stephen Essex of
Plymouth University should all receive special mention.
Julie and James are my constant support.

The illustrations on pages 20, 26 and 42 are courtesy of
Getty Images, and that on page 14 is courtesy of Sport
& General.

IMPERIAL WAR MUSEUM COLLECTIONS
Some of the photos in this book come from the Imperial
War Museum's huge collections which cover all aspects of
conflict involving Britain and the Commonwealth since the
start of the twentieth century. These rich resources are
available online to search, browse and buy at
www.iwmcollections.org.uk. In addition to Collections
Online, you can visit the Visitor Rooms where you can
explore over 8 million photographs, thousands of hours of
moving images, the largest sound archive of its kind in the
world, thousands of diaries and letters written by people
in wartime, and a huge reference library. To make an
appointment, call (020) 7416 5320, or e-mail
mail@iwm.org.uk. Imperial War Museum
www.iwm.org.uk

Shire Publications is supporting the Woodland Trust, the UK's leading woodland conservation charity, by funding the dedication of trees.

CONTENTS

PRELUDE   4

THE BLITZ BEGINS   16

THE BLITZ INTENSIFIES   26

REVENGE   42

AFTERMATH   50

FURTHER READING   55

INDEX   56

AIR RAIDS

COMPLETELY RE-WRITTEN

1941

3d.

WHAT YOU MUST KNOW
WHAT YOU MUST DO!

PRELUDE

T HE BLITZ – what does it mean to us now? The most intensive aerial
bombardments of civilian centres then known, the assault on Britain
during 1940–1 has come to represent a symbol of endurance. Though more
concentrated attacks have destroyed cities and devastated populations since
then, London, the ports and the industrial centres of Britain received some
of the most sustained aerial campaigns ever to have been meted out on the
cities of Europe – and the strongest experienced up until then. Named the
'Blitz' after the success of the German strategy of the rapid 'lightning war',
or *Blitzkrieg*, which swept aside the European nations in 1939–40, it has
become a watchword for both devastation and human fortitude in adversity.

The 'spirit of the Blitz' – the endurance and togetherness of the ordinary
people of Britain who faced the bombing – has been challenged by some
revisionists, who point to the numbers who fled the bombed cities nightly,
the miscellany of crimes carried out in the blackout, the looting of bombed
houses and war profiteering. That such things were to occur is understandable
(and equally so, that they were 'covered up' during the war itself for the sake
of 'morale'); it is more surprising, surely, that people did endure, and that
despite the shocks, were capable of returning to the war effort daily up and
down the country. Thus despite the efforts of some to downgrade the
togetherness of the British people at one of their most challenging times in
history, the evidence of commentators at the time indicates otherwise. In his
book *Living Through the Blitz*, Tom Harrisson, one of the originators of Mass
Observation (an organisation of volunteers set up in 1937 to record public
opinion during an uncertain time for world peace) commented: 'Whatever it
did destroy, it failed over any period of more than days appreciably to diminish
the human will, or at least the capacity to endure.'

The purpose of this volume is to give an introduction to a complex and
well-studied subject in a simple and concise volume. For some purists, 'The
Blitz' refers only to the bombing of 1940–1; this book will explore the
prelude to aerial attack, the main Blitz on British cities, the revenge attacks
on historic targets and the V-weapons offensives. It will also examine the role

Opposite:
Air Raids – Many
booklets were
produced by the
Ministry of Home
Security to
prepare Britain
to receive air
attack. This one,
published in 1941,
learns from the
experience of the
raids of 1940.

Right: *Hitler Passed this Way* is typical of books that were commercially produced during the war, depicting the bomb damage wrought on Britain during the Blitz.

Far right: *War Factory* – one of many reports on the state of the nation's war effort by the social recording volunteers, Mass Observation.

of the unarmed 'citizen army' that supported the people in their travail, and discuss ultimately the triumph of the nation under extreme adversity.

ORIGINS

London had been under aerial attack before; it had experienced raids from Imperial Germany during the First World War, with Zeppelin 'baby killers' (from January 1915) and twin-engined Gotha bombers (from Spring 1917). With little direct prospect of victory, and with increasing desperation, these weapons were flung across the English Channel, attacking primarily the capital and its surroundings. These early air raids caused widespread fear and dismay among the civilian population, which gathered under railway arches and massed at underground stations as a means of escape – an act to be repeated in the later war. In all, 1,413 people were killed and 3,409 injured; a paltry number by Second World War standards, but significant all the same. Critically, analysis of the effects of these raids would provide the basis of post-war predictions of future aerial campaigns – as well as the first introduction of countermeasures, such as barrage balloons, fighter aircraft and anti-aircraft guns.

In the prelude to war, many academics challenged the Government's assumptions, and predicted mass deaths from future bombing. Books like these offer criticism of the policies – but not necessarily solutions.

The further refinement of aerial bombardment can be traced to an Italian military theorist, Guilio Douhet, who viewed the attrition of civilian targets as an effective means of prosecuting war – his theories developed from experience of the First World War. They would be put to the test during the widening of Italian territorial ambitions in Africa – with aerial bombing and the deployment of gas in Abyssinia in 1935. In the light of this and other campaigns waged during the fragile, post-war world, with mounting hysteria, shrill academic voices were raised to warn of the future onslaught Britain would face in the advent of war. And Sylvia Pankhurst, former suffragette and peace activist, would raise the first 'anti-war memorial' outside her home – a 'stone bomb', which sits incongruously today within a leafy, tranquil, Essex suburb.

According to the predictions, vast aerial armadas would destroy cities with high explosives and target the civilian populations with gas; casualties would be enormous, civil authorities would be overwhelmed; cities would be razed to the ground. Extrapolation led the Government to consider that 120,000 casualties were to be a likely result of a single week's bombing of Britain. Such opinions gained credence following the devastating German-led bombing of Spanish cities during the Civil War of 1936–7 (recorded in such powerful works as Picasso's *Guernica*, 1937). 'The bomber would always get through', the words of Prime Minister Stanley Baldwin, became the mantra of the pre-war peace movement in Britain.

Sylvia Pankhurst's 'anti-war memorial', a stone bomb set up on her property in Woodford Green, Essex, in 1935. Its suburban situation is incongruous now.

In this way, the bombing of Britain in 1940 was expected as an inevitability; fleets of bombers would wreak havoc with the major cities and industrialised areas of the United Kingdom. The policy of appeasement of Hitler and his regime was intended to avert war – or to delay at it least; with the Munich Agreement of September 1938, Neville Chamberlain signed away the sovereignty of Czechoslovakia, with the faint hope of quenching Hitler's thirst for war. It failed. After Munich, and Hitler's broken 'promises' made on that 'scrap of paper', Britain was heading inevitably and inexorably for war.

AIR DEFENCE

Rearmament was of prime importance, and equipping the Royal Air Force (RAF) with the tools to attack the bombers was clearly of the greatest significance. Yet, in the false peace following the defeat of Germany in 1918, the defence of Britain was a low priority. While in 1918 Britain could boast 286 anti-aircraft guns (or 'Ack-Ack', after the phonetic spelling of 'AA') and 387 searchlights protecting its capital city, by 1920, this number had declined to zero. Still, the changing world order demanded that Britain consider once

A contemporary postcard showing one of Britain's 3.7-inch anti-aircraft guns.

more its defences in the light of new threats. The joint RAF/Army Steel-Bartholomew Committee identified the three components of Britain's defensive strategy: first, that the RAF should receive advance warning of attack in order to reach its fighting height; second, that ground defences were essential to protect vulnerable points, particularly ports, and other transport nodes; and third, that information on the movement of aircraft must be gained and disseminated quickly.

Warning of the bombers approaching the coast was to be provided by both the top secret innovation, the Chain Home (CH) system (radar as it became known), and the more down-to-earth, but still vital, spotters of the Observer Corps – necessary as radar could not detect enemy raiders once they passed over land. By 1938 the Corps had established a network of posts in south and eastern England, later expanded to cover the rest of the country. From these often-isolated posts, observers strained with their eyes and ears to determine the altitude, direction and number of enemy raiders. These daylight raiders would then be met by RAF fighters. Detecting night bombers and knocking them from the sky at the height of the Blitz was an all together more challenging task. Thanks to Britain's radar, Observer Corps and roof spotters, the approach of raiders during the intensive blitz periods was nearly always well advertised. Raiders were mostly preceded by the distinctive wailing of wartime air raid sirens, still one of the most recognisable sounds, even today. There was an urgency to the sound, warning the public to head for their shelters, and for the various civil defence organisations to ready themselves.

Part of the aerial defence of Britain was the deployment of tethered 'barrage balloons' under the control of RAF Balloon Command, established in 1938. These 65-foot-long silver 'gas bags' (designated Low Zone or LZ balloons) were to become a familiar sight in wartime Britain, and were used widely to protect vulnerable cities, ports and industry by forcing bombers to fly higher than their altitude of 5,000 feet. (The balloon tethers also included fiendish parachute devices designed to stall enemy aircraft if they were unfortunate enough to hit them.) The balloon barrage would reduce the accuracy of the bombing, as well as forcing the bombers to fly at an optimum altitude for anti-aircraft fire, as AA guns were less effective against lower flying aircraft. Here, searchlights, also deployed by the RAF, would comb the skies for enemy raiders. By the middle of 1940 there were 1,400 balloons, a third of them over the London area.

The anti-aircraft gun defences were to be gradually built up throughout the early part of the war, with twelve divisions of the army's Anti-Aircraft Command (under General Frederick Pile) crewing the guns and searchlights. These divisions were regionally distributed to afford maximum protection, but the amount available was inadequate for the task ahead; in 1939 there was less than one-fifth of the actual requirement available. Yet, despite this, AA guns served an important task. Though knocking enemy aircraft from the skies was obviously the desired result, AA fire was also to drive the enemy higher in the sky. Gun aiming was the biggest problem, however; this was not satisfactorily resolved until the widespread use of radar-aiming technology later on in the war.

Famously, on 10 September 1940 'every gun was to fire every possible round' into the sky with the opening of 'the London Barrage' – massed gunnery that, though inaccurate, was to drive the Blitz attackers higher into the inky night sky, and increase the confidence of the beleaguered Londoners. There were negative side-effects, though, as Denis Gardner remembered:

Above: Postcards illustrating the 'gas bags' of RAF Balloon Command, operated by the Women's Auxiliary Air Force, the WAAF.

An air raid is horrific, not just from the bombs but also from the anti-aircraft guns that make a terrible noise, and the shrapnel that rains down afterwards. Also lots of our own shells came down and exploded on contact with the ground.

Right:
A child's biscuit tin collection of shrapnel, bomb parts and other war souvenirs, all labelled. Collecting fever was rife among children in the Blitz.

Though dangerous, such shards would nevertheless be collected avidly by eager schoolchildren, who would brave the bombs to gain their prizes. Contemporary experts were scornful of the value of the AA barrage, estimating that as many as 3,000 shells would be needed to have only one-fiftieth of a chance of hitting one aircraft travelling at 250 mph. Despite this, the role of AA Command was never to slacken during the war, and new methods were needed to try and shoot down flying bombs during the V-weapon offensives of 1944.

PASSIVE DEFENCE

In 1924, the Committee of Imperial Defence set up a subcommittee to consider issues of civil defence, then called 'Air Raid Precautions' or 'ARP' under senior civil servant Sir John Anderson. This was to become the basis of the more formal Air Raid Precautions Department, which from 1 April 1935 directed the development of passive air defence in Britain, a direct response to the announcement by Germany in 1935 that it possessed an air force – in direct violation of the terms of the Versailles Treaty.

An ARP Rescue Squad, c. 1940. The ARP services would be well trained and highly effective during the war.

The Government's approach to ARP was regional, based on twelve civil defence regions, and inherently local, with ARP Wardens providing the link between the public and the Government. On the advent of war, the overall direction for ARP services passed to a new ministry – the Ministry of Home

Security, which would administer its actions through a regional structure, with ten regions in England (the most populous country), and one each for Scotland and Wales. The ARP services were locally recruited, with several specialist branches: Wardens, Rescue, Gas Decontamination, Ambulance, First Aid, all coordinated by a Report and Control Service, itself informed by Messengers. These services would be required to deal, on an intimate, street-by-street basis, with the citizens of Britain, guiding them, assisting them, and, when the time came, helping to rescue them from danger.

The ARP lapel badge, worn by the men and women of the service before the issue of uniform in 1941.

The Air Raid Precautions Act of 1937 consolidated the relationship between the Government's plans, and the responsibility of local government and the average citizen in providing for their own safety in wartime. On 1 January 1938, the new Act came into force, compelling local authorities to take action to recruit, set up and train their ARP services. Initial reactions to the new ARP service were at best lukewarm, and at worst hostile. The majority of ARP workers were part-timers, working a maximum of 48 hours a month, with full-time personnel paid at a rate of £3 a week for men (and £2 a week for women) – earning them, and their fellow volunteers in the Auxiliary Fire Service, the undeserved name of 'three-quid-a-week army dodgers'. Such names fell away with the first fall of bombs on the towns and cities of Britain.

PREPARING FOR ARMAGEDDON

With dire predictions of inner cities razed by bombers within hours, and local authorities struggling to cope with thousands of casualties, central to the Government's thoughts was the evacuation of the vulnerable when war threatened. Fearing that war would bring immediate bombing and gas attacks, the Government had made plans for the priority evacuation of mothers, children and the disabled from vulnerable areas. A million and a quarter people were to be moved out of the capital, including the pupils and staff of entire schools, and into reception areas across the south, East Anglia and the Midlands. In practice, about 600,000 actually left as part of 'Operation Pied Piper' in August/September 1939 and many of these had returned by the Christmas as the uneventful 'Phoney War' lulled parents into a false sense of security. In many cases, evacuees returned home before the bombs began to fall. Other evacuations followed the fall of France, the onset of the Blitz in Autumn 1940 and during the V-bomb offensives in 1944, but it was this initial exodus that posed the greatest logistical challenge and which has lodged so vividly in popular memory.

Luminous Blackout jewellery was just one of the many innovations from the period; the Blackout was total, and 'seeing and being seen' was important when vehicles still used the roads.

LUMINOUS JEWE
FOR BLACK OUT

BRITISH MADE

With the introduction of the ARP Act came provision for the introduction of lighting restrictions. If there was one

The sound of the air raid siren is familiar even now; it had to be tested before the war to acclimatise people to its purpose.

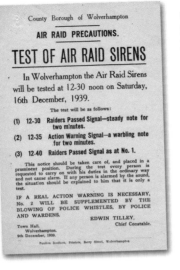

County Borough of Wolverhampton

AIR RAID PRECAUTIONS.

TEST OF AIR RAID SIRENS

In Wolverhampton the Air Raid Sirens will be tested at 12-30 noon on Saturday, 16th December, 1939.

The test will be as follows:

(1) 12-30 Raiders Passed Signal—steady note for two minutes.

(2) 12-35 Action Warning Signal—a warbling note for two minutes.

(3) 12-40 Raiders Passed Signal as at No. 1.

This notice should be taken care of, and placed in a prominent position. During the test every person is requested to carry on with his duties in the ordinary way and not cause alarm. If any person is alarmed by the sound, the situation should be explained to him that it is only a test.

IF A REAL ACTION WARNING IS NECESSARY, No. 2 WILL BE SUPPLEMENTED BY THE BLOWING OF POLICE WHISTLES, BY POLICE AND WARDENS.

EDWIN TILLEY,
Chief Constable.

Town Hall,
Wolverhampton.
9th December, 1939.

Poulton Brothers, Printers, Berry Street, Wolverhampton.

aspect above all other that dominates the whole war experience on the Home Front, it is that of the 'Blackout'. Difficult to appreciate by those who have not been through it – the official historian himself could only describe it as 'having to be seen to be believed' – its introduction was to cause the first civilian casualties of the war, before any bombs had even been dropped. Universally disliked, it was introduced just before the outbreak of war, on 1 September 1939. The Blackout was intended to reduce the target for enemy bombers, and was vigorously enforced. Londoner Dobbie Dobinson recalls, 'The Blackout became a necessary evil and enthusiastic air raid wardens left you in no doubt as to the consequences of allowing even a chink of light to escape from your windows. These men were eventually to prove real heroes, when raids became a reality.' Actually, one in six wardens would be women. The Blackout would be total in the early stages of the war.

People in Muswell Hill, London, take delivery of their Anderson shelter components on 27 February 1939. (IWM HU 36151)

If the Blackout was to hinder night raiders, the air raid warning system was meant to announce their coming – loudly. Decided upon by the ARP Committee well in advance of war, the electrically-driven factory sirens were chosen and placed strategically so that the maximum number of people could hear them. With the potential for false alarms, the operation of air raid sirens was initially the responsibility of the Police. Once information was received from Fighter Command of an impending raid, a 'Preliminary Caution' ('Air Raid Message – Yellow') would be issued by telephone, providing fifteen minutes' warning, followed by the 'Action Warning' ('Air Raid Warning – Red'), with five minutes. A further alert, 'Air Raid Warning – Purple', was be added in 1940 as a means of reducing the interruption to industry. Once notice had been given of 'Raiders Passed' ('Air Raid Message – Green'), the sirens would once more be sounded – this time a continuous two-minute signal of steady pitch.

With the announcement of the arrival of raiders, it was expected that people would take refuge in air raid shelters. Yet the Government's policy had been made plain before the war: no deep shelters would be provided. They would be costly and time consuming to build; in order to be effective they would need to be within a 300-yard radius of at least 6,000–7,000 people. And, it was argued, once safe underground, a 'shelter mentality' might affect the nation, to the detriment of the war effort – promoting absenteeism from work. The Government was anxious that sheltering would best be done at home, the population dispersed and not a target for high explosive (HE) bombs. As such it planned for the distribution of what it termed 'Galvanised Steel Shelters' – later to become universally known as 'Anderson' shelters.

The Anderson shelter was named after its inventor, Dr David Anderson. It was to become the core of the Government's shelter policy. Six feet high, and taking up an area of 6' 6" ′ 4' 6", the Anderson shelter was delivered from storage at railway yards, consisting of corrugated steel sheets weighing 8 cwt. It was to be sited in a pit dug between 3 feet and 4 feet deep, and covered with earth – a valuable plot for growing vegetables. The shelters were

Diagram of the component parts of an Anderson shelter, from the Government's official guide to their construction.

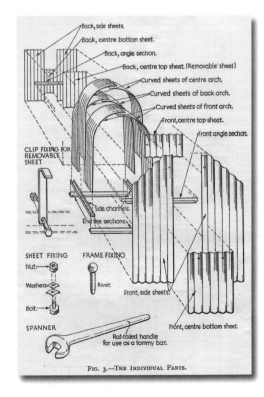

FIG. 3.—THE INDIVIDUAL PARTS.

delivered by councils as fourteen separate galvanised panels, together with assorted bolts, as Betty Balfour of Crewe remembers:

> There was an assortment of sheets of bright new corrugated iron, long straight pieces, short straight pieces. All the curved ones were long and they were the most awkward to handle. There was a bag made of sacking which held nuts and bolts which should correspond with the holes in the corrugated sheets. No sign of any instruction or diagram.

The Anderson took some time to site properly.

Although untested when first delivered, the Andersons were shown later to be able to withstand falling masonry from the average house, and to be proof from the blast of a 500-pound bomb to a distance of 30 feet. In fact, it was proof against closer shaves than that, and many families had cause to thank its resilience in battle. Andersons were distributed free to those on low incomes, and 2.3 million examples were eventually distributed. In 1941, bulky steel cage 'Morrison' shelters, designed to take the weight of a collapsed domestic building, were available to those who had no garden.

Dispersal of the population to domestic shelters was the backbone of the Government's shelter policy, but it was recognised that, in many cases, there was no alternative but to create public shelters – for those caught in raids away from home, and for those living in communal buildings and flats. Trenches had originally been dug in public parks and green spaces following Munich; most communal shelters were built on the surface. Brick built (with often shoddy materials), and concrete roofed, such shelters were sometimes referred to as 'Morrison sandwiches' – a reference to the potential for roof collapse onto the shelterers below, named unkindly after the then Home

A surface air raid shelter ('Morrison Sandwich'), in south-east London. They were not popular, despite the cheery message. (IWM HU 36246)

Secretary, Herbert Morrison. Local authorities were to designate appropriate buildings and underground spaces as public shelters, and, in some rare cases, natural and historic tunnels and caves were identified as shelter spaces.

The London Underground had never figured in the Government's shelter policy. Those who looked to the safety of the 'Tube', as they had during the First World War, looked initially in vain: in the view of the ARP Committee, the Underground would be needed for the transport of essential supplies, for the evacuation of the many casualties expected when the bombing started and to enable the hub of the Empire to continue to function. But Londoners thought differently, and those who had no choice but to seek refuge in public or communal shelters were quick to criticise the brick-and-concrete surface shelters as unsafe and unsavoury. Although the London Passenger Transport Board, under instruction from above, tried to stop Londoners seeking refuge on the platforms, a minor revolt outside Liverpool Street Station in the heart of the City of London on 7 September 1940 – the beginning of the Blitz proper – saw stations opened finally to the shelterers, the Home Office switching to a system of regulated use. At first, facilities were poor, but these were quickly improved, with the provision of sanitation, catering and bunks. At first, 'getting a pitch' was rather hit and miss; people had to queue hours before the stations opened for shelter at 4 p.m., and unscrupulous touts known as 'droppers' hired their services to reserve spaces for paying customers. From November 1940, local authorities allocated shelter tickets to their residents, tied to a particular tube station, and a particular numbered pitch within it. These were issued for a set period, during which a shelterer could use the station each night, after 6.30 p.m. In addition, subject to space being available, individuals could apply to the station ticket office on a given day for a casual ticket to shelter that night. At the height of the Blitz on London, the Tube accommodated 177,000 people – only 4 per cent of central Londoners, many of whom left the city to seek shelter or refuge elsewhere, 27 per cent of them to the humble Anderson shelter.

When the bombing of British cities finally arrived in the summer of 1940, there was little surprise; the Battle of Britain had raged for almost two months. In the thick of things, the ARP and fire services battled the incendiary-bomb driven fires that raged through city centres across Britain in the summer–autumn period of 1940–1. The people's response to their initial baptism of fire was recorded by Mass Observation: when the first bombs fell there was widespread fear; after the initial shock there was resignation to what was to become a 'new code of living'. And with this code came the recognition that Britain 'could take it'.

Ticket issued to a local resident for Elephant and Castle tube station, one of many used as air raid shelters late in 1940.

LUFTWAFFE
über dem Feind

THE BLITZ BEGINS

AFTER THE DECLARATION OF WAR on 3 September 1939, the anticipated aerial onslaught failed to materialise; yet almost immediately after Neville Chamberlain's historic radio broadcast at 11 a.m. that fateful Sunday morning, the air raid sirens were to sound in earnest for the first time. Mass Observation was on hand. On an individual level, reaction was varied. How else would the public deal with a new phenomenon? Though the Government had bombarded the public with leaflets and guidance pamphlets, that the distinctive wailing sound should be heard so early portended doom, the doom predicted by pre-war intelligentsia. This 'September siren shock' highlighted to many their unpreparedness. Air Raid Wardens bustled in the street; householders searched for their gas masks and anti-gas tape; people rushed about frantically unknowing. This early warning was triggered by nothing more than a stray, lone aircraft. But it was a valuable lesson, and the British people would learn quickly.

The first actual bombs on British soil landed in Hoy, Orkney in October 1939; the first civilian killed by bombing was also in Orkney, six months after the outbreak of war, on 16 March 1940. Bombing of mainland Britain – in Kent and northeast England – came in May, with the first daylight attacks in July. In August, many cities received their first taste of the war, often as desultory raids aimed mostly at ports, industry and transport links. Portsmouth – home of the Royal Navy – was to receive its first raid on 11 July, and the raids that followed during August were among the heaviest to be experienced outside London in the earliest part of the Blitz. The city was very much in the front line with Hitler's planned invasion of Britain still on the cards. Unlike what was to come, these raids were mostly in daylight, with under a hundred bombers per raid, but with Portsmouth's unique geography on a peninsula between two great natural harbours, it was not hard to pick out a target. The damage was extensive. Many other cities would receive similar attention.

The attacks on Portsmouth and other cities abated when in September London was targeted – with fifty-seven consecutive nights of bombing.

Opposite:
Luftwaffe über dem Feind (Luftwaffe over the enemy). This book, published in Berlin in 1941, celebrates the 'successes' of the German bombers across Europe in 1939–40, including London and Coventry, and illustrates a Ju88 in action.

Stürm vor England's Toren (Storm before England's gates). German pamphlet published after Dunkirk, June 1940 – predicting the future invasion of the British Isles.

Air raid damage in south-west London, August 1940. Many cities would receive attention from German bombers during the prelude to the Blitz proper, opening on 7 September 1940. (IWM HU 26247)

From then on, the bombers searched out new targets, and discovered new ways of hitting them hard. In the ensuing months, the services of all the major towns and cities throughout the United Kingdom were severely stretched, as they suffered their own intense period of blitz.

In fact, the term 'Blitz', as commonly understood, was the sustained period of bombing of Britain's cities from September 1940 through to May 1941. Yet attacks of one kind or another continued throughout the war. Commencement of the Blitz followed on from the failure of Göring's policy of destroying airbases and ports in preparation for Operation *Sealion* – the invasion of Britain. Bombing was concentrated, but at first steered well away from London – the biggest target of all – on the express orders of Hitler. Fatefully, during a German air raid on Thames Haven and Purfleet on 24 August 1940, the first bombs were to fall on the capital. Bombers from this flight had strayed off target, and had released their bombs on the city, predominantly over the East End and north London. With the first bombs on the capital so began the escalation of the aerial campaign; the RAF would bomb Berlin the next evening. On 25 August, eighty RAF bombers targeted the Nazi capital; only half reached their target. There was very little damage – yet Göring had already promised that not a single enemy bomber would appear over the Fatherland, and Hitler was to call for comprehensive retaliatory action against British cities. Famously, at Berlin's Sportplatz on 4 September, he promised, 'If they attack our cities, we shall raze theirs to the ground'. He also pledged a hundred bombs in return for every bomb dropped on Germany. With this, and with the Battle of Britain still at its height, Göring's sights moved to London, away from Fighter Command. On 7 September, the Luftwaffe's bombers were turned away from the ports and airfields targeted as part of the preparations for the invasion of Britain, and were refocused on the capital – the Battle of London had begun. At a time when the RAF was almost at the end of its resources, the airfields were left alone – buying crucial time for the beleaguered fighters. The Battle of Britain would be won by the RAF on 15 September.

That London was targeted on that fateful Saturday has much to do with revenge, and for Göring this was to be an historic day. With London deliberately targeted on the afternoon of 7 September 1940, the Port of London – the rambling docks and harbours concentrated along the Thames as it snaked its way through the packed residential areas of London's East End – was the main focus of the attack. Flying at first in daylight, and then at night, the Luftwaffe was to hit London hard. A concentrated force of 364 bombers made the attack, with substantial fighter support; they were fiercely opposed by RAF Fighter Command, who, though worn from the weeks of opposing the Luftwaffe campaigns attacking ports and airfields, were ready to accept this new responsibility. At 4.56 p.m., the sirens were sounded that presaged the attack, warning Londoners to take shelter. And from 5 p.m., the German bombers appeared over the city – large numbers of high-explosive bombs were unloaded on the docks and city areas. Limehouse, Millwall and Surrey Docks were all targeted, as would be the Woolwich Arsenal just to the south of the Thames. All of these targets could claim to have some element of military legitimacy; but packed tightly with the industrial areas were

Blitz fires in
London:
September 1940.

thousands of dwelling houses, and thousands of civilians – civilians who would be the victims of the bombs. Further to the east, West Ham power station and Beckton gasworks would also be hit, while the bombers also made their way to Westminster and Kensington.

Bill Killick lived in Bermondsey, close to the Thames and within sight of the docks:

I can well remember the first daylight raid of the Blitz, watching the bombers high up in the sky over Bermondsey, with the vapour trails going in and out of the bombers, these must have been the fighter planes of the RAF, although we couldn't identify them. I remember hearing the bombs raining down, and the succession of explosions, in sticks of five or six I think, if they were getting louder they were coming towards us and softer, away from us. Later in the afternoon we watched the great clouds of black smoke plume towards the sky with a warm orange glow beneath them.

The enemy would attack at night too, returning at 8 p.m. after a break of just two hours with a force just over a third of the size of that which had attacked during the day. The attack would continue into the early morning hours; the effect was devastating. The port areas were vulnerable: warehouses packed with flammable materials were set alight, burning through into the evening and acting as a beacon for the second wave of bombers that would attack at night. London's fire services struggled to deal with this concerted attack.

Guided by the flames the bombers pounded London with high explosives. Surrounding the docks and industrial areas targeted by the Luftwaffe, thousands of homes were destroyed or damaged beyond repair; mainline stations were rendered useless and vessels in the bustling Thames basin were sunk, burned or bombed. Many of the fires were burning out of control, forming huge areas of spreading flame; there were nine of these, one of them at the Surrey Docks, storage for 1.5 million tons of soft woods imported from the Baltic. Over an area of 250 acres these resinous woods were burning, stacked in piles 20 feet high, the heat so intense that the paving was alight. There were many such stories from that raid. Surveying the scene was the regional fire officer for London, Sir Aylmer Firebrace:

> The fires in the vicinity of the Royal Albert and King George V Docks were an awe-inspiring sight; the situation was completely out of hand. Superstructures of ships were blazing; acres of warehouses were on fire from end to end; molten tar was flowing alight over many of the roads, often filling bomb craters with liquid fire.

In all, 436 Londoners would be killed, and 1,666 injured from this raid.

In the days that followed, the bombers returned by night. The damage wrought on 7 September would be repeated again on Sunday 8 September. The respite from daylight bombing was a relief, but at 7.30 p.m. two hundred aircraft appeared over the east of the city to blast away at the same targets; this time there were twelve major conflagrations, and all rail transport links to the south of the capital were severed; another 412 Londoners were killed

that night, and 747 seriously wounded. London was clearly going to be the centre of Göring's attention for some time.

The response of many was to flee the East End as urban refugees: to the east was the green sward of Epping Forest, spreading from Leytonstone northeastwards into Essex. Others headed west, seeking out deep shelters beneath public buildings, in church crypts or department store

Shelter signs still point passers-by to vaults in Great North Street, Westminster. West End shelters were sought out by people fleeing the East End in September 1940.

basements. And even more pressing were the crowds that gathered at the underground stations. The safety of some of these were illusory; there were to be several bomb-induced disasters, with appalling loss of life, at these sanctuaries. The official view of these migrations was one of some alarm; but this pattern was to be observed in later blitzes in other towns – and for the most part, the people returned to their jobs, their homes, their neighbourhoods, and Britain 'carried on'.

For the average Londoner, sleep deprivation during the September Blitz and beyond was to be a major problem. Retiring to their cramped Andersons, the crowded platforms of the tubes, or even the foetid squalor of some communal surface shelters, the throb of the bombers, the cacophony of the falling bombs and the crack of the answering AA guns, meant that sleep was fitful, if attained at all. The night raiders would test the morale of the nation severely.

In order to enact the loud promises of destruction made by both Göring and Hitler, between a hundred and two hundred bombers attacked London every night but one between mid-September and mid-November. These bombers destroyed houses and people's lives; they severed transport links

and damaged war production. But all of these were temporary. London carried on. Shop fronts were emblazoned with chalked messages, such as 'more open than usual' or 'Hitler can't stop us'. That 5,730 people were killed and 10,000 were badly injured was an inescapable fact of the bombing campaign; but there can be no doubt that Londoners endured.

By mid-November, the Germans had dropped more than 13,000 tons of high-explosive bombs and more than one million incendiary bombs on London. Unopposed other than the then ineffective 'barrage' of anti-aircraft guns, and by largely obsolete aircraft pressed into service as 'catseye' night fighters – relying on nerve and nous but lacking all-important radar at this early part of the war – the Luftwaffe would suffer losses of only 1 per cent by combat casualties. More would be lost in accidents and mechanical failure than would be shot down; new technology was needed to effectively combat the attackers.

A typical Blitz street scene in Limehouse; 'bombed but not beaten'. (IWM HU 103762)

THE RAIDERS

The Luftwaffe was organised into *Luftflotten* (air fleets) directed by the High Command of the Luftwaffe (Oberkommando der Luftwaffe). Each air fleet would have a range of tactical squadrons at its disposal, and would have fighter

General-
feldmarschall Hugo
Sperrle, architect
of the Blitz on
Britain.

aircraft, bombers, anti-aircraft provisions and even paratroops under its control. Luftflotte 3, commanded by Generalfeldmarschall Hugo Sperrle from 1939 to 1944, was responsible for supplying bombers and fighter support during the attacks on London and the other towns and cities to follow. Divided into *Geschwader*, most bombers would be grouped into *Kampfgeschwader* ('bomber wings'), and many would be based in northern Europe, facing Britain. Specialist independent bomb groups, called *Kampfgruppen*, were also used, often as pathfinders equipped with the latest equipment, their purpose to light the target with incendiaries. One at least, Kampfgruppe 100, was to attain fame and notoriety for its raids on the British mainland in 1940–1, seeing action in the fire-bombing of Coventry, Manchester and London in late 1940.

Though arguably under-engined and under-armed, the German bombers were capable of accurate navigation, thanks to a suite of devices that allowed the bombers to detect focused radio waves beamed in the direction of its target. The first of these, '*Knickebein*' ('bent leg'), used an overlapping system of radio waves that would give a signal of morse dots (to the left) or morse dashes (to the right) that would coalesce to form a continuous tone at its centre. This could give a theoretical accuracy for the beam of one-seventh of a degree, so accurate that it could place bombers over their target within one kilometre. Discovered by the British in spring 1940, Dr R. V. Jones of the Air Ministry Scientific Intelligence Service was to develop an antidote: a beam (code-named 'Aspirin') that overlaid *Knickebein* (code-named 'Headache') and created confusion. *Knickebein* would be improved upon in August 1940, in time for the assault on London. The mysteriously named '*X-Verfahren*' ('X-procedure') would employ intersecting beams (picked up by aircraft equipped with the *X-Gerät* – the X-device) that would provide the possibility of $300m^2$ accuracy – the size of a single building. Though the British were able to counter this too (with 'bromide'), the pathfinder *Kampfgruppen* would use it to good effect.

The bombers flown by the German bombing units were well known to British observers, who had been trained to spot their distinctive shapes and profiles using recognition books and cards. German bombers were hampered by their relative lack of defensive armament, and by their reliance on twin engines – the RAF would use hardier four-engined aircraft during its assault on the Fatherland. Distinctive was the whale-like Heinkel He 111, with its rounded plexiglass nose; and the longer, slimmer and faster 'wonder-bomber', the Junkers Ju 88. Bomb loads would also be limited: 2,000 kg for

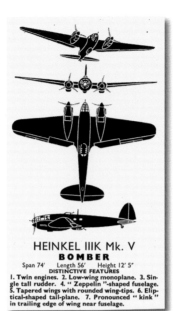

JUNKERS Ju. 88 (JUMO 211)
LONG RANGE BOMBER
Span 59'   Length 46' 6'   Height 15'
DISTINCTIVE FEATURES
1. Twin engines. 2. Low-wing monoplane. 3. Bulbous nose and slim long fuselage. 4. Single large rudder. 5. Wings sharply tapered towards ends. 6. Tail-plane set well forward.

HEINKEL IIIK Mk. V
BOMBER
Span 74'   Length 56'   Height 12' 5'
DISTINCTIVE FEATURES
1. Twin engines. 2. Low-wing monoplane. 3. Single tall rudder. 4. " Zeppelin "-shaped fuselage. 5. Tapered wings with rounded wing-tips. 6. Eliptical-shaped tail-plane. 7. Pronounced " kink " in trailing edge of wing near fuselage.

Far left: Junkers Ju 88, the 'wonder bomber', and one of the mainstays of Luftflotte 3. A page from an aircraft spotter's handbook, 1940.

Left: Heinkel He 111, the main aircraft of Kampfgruppe 100, the pathfinders. A page from an aircraft spotter's handbook, 1940.

the He 111; 2,500 kg for the Ju 88. The main bombs carried by these aircraft were high explosive and designated *sprengbombe-cylindrisch*, or SC, and eight out of ten bombs dropped by the Luftwaffe over Britain were of this type, with a size range of 50–2,000 kg. The larger bombs had names like 'Hermann' (SC 1000), 'Satan' (SC 1800) and 'Max' (SC 2500), the latter the largest of its type dropped during the Blitz. These bombs could be fitted with impact or delayed action fuses.

Other large bombs were dropped by parachute; these were sea mines dropped on land. Sadly, these were often taken for descending aircrew or paratroopers, and those rushing to capture them were most often killed outright from the blast. Devastating, these *Luftmines* were in two weights, 500 kg and 1,000 kg. Common were the incendiary bombs (*Brandebomben*) that were dropped in containers known to the British as 'Molotov Breadbaskets'. The main types were the 1 kg and 2 kg 'electron' bomb; these were magnesium bodied with a thermite core that would be set alight on impact, and would be a devil of a job to extinguish once they had taken hold, burning at over 3,000°C. Larger 'oil bombs' would help spread the fires. The main weapon of 'Fire Bomb Fritz' in late 1940–1, this weapon would force the hand of British civil defences after the fire bombing of British cities in late 1940, with the invention of a new service, the Fire Guard. Almost everyone was eligible to join its ranks – but until then, Britons would have to endure the firestorm.

THE BLITZ INTENSIFIES

FOLLOWING the attacks of August and the September Blitz of London, a nightly routine emerged. A typical air raid over Britain in 1940–1 was at night (full-scale daylight raids were abandoned by the Luftwaffe by October), and involved up to two hundred bombers, but often more than twice that number, dropping both explosive and incendiary bombs. In September 1940, London, principal target of the Luftwaffe, received 5,300 bombs alone – some inner boroughs receiving up to one hundred bombs per square mile. In all, 18,800 HE bombs would be dropped during 71 raids on the capital in 1940–1.

The raid on Coventry on 14 November, one of the heaviest of the war – it lasted for ten hours and involved a concentrated attack of five hundred bombers on a considerably smaller target than London – saw 500 tons of high explosive and 900 tons of incendiaries dropped. By May 1941, 43,000 people had been killed in air raids, and 1.4 million had been made homeless.

Reactions to the bombing varied. Tom Harrisson, leading Mass Observation, recorded the views of bombed civilians, and noted a typical pattern. At first, within minutes, there was shock; usually manifested in barked orders and incessant chatter. Typically, within hours there would be some recovery, with emotions and concern for others re-emerging; this would be followed by a desire to relive the moment, discussing with anyone who would listen the minutiae of their 'incident'. Within days, pride would appear, a pride born from knowing that they had survived whatever Hitler could throw at them – followed quickly by a return to the norm, a norm characterised by grumbling, but underlined by a concern for others. This sequence – easily understandable – must surely be a root of the 'Blitz spirit' of Londoners and others who had suffered bombing raids.

Knowing what to do after the raiders had passed was essential, especially when, emerging from your garden Anderson shelter, your home was in ruins. The Ministry of Home Security *After the Raid* leaflets of December 1940 commenced with the soothing words, 'When you have been in the front line and taken it extra hard the country wants to look after you'. The leaflets

Opposite:
The City ablaze: fires blazed out of control during the 'Second Great Fire of London', December 1940.

Right: *London Blitzed Again!* German propaganda leaflet dropped over Britain.

Far right: *After the Raid*, Government advice for Blitz victims, 1940.

provided advice on where to go for help, shelter and food, and how to go about getting help for people to repair their homes. Part of that advice was the attendance at Rest Centres, set up by local authorities, and staffed in many cases by the Women's Voluntary Service (WVS). These centres were an important component of the Government's civil defence strategy, providing, as was intended, the first port of call for bombed-out civilians in need of a place to seek refuge, to sleep, and to receive a meal and a hot drink – the all-important cup of tea. The quality of provision varied according to location; but regardless of this there would be comfort from the shock of being made instantly homeless, with the loss of relatives and friends.

The shock of losing one's home to the Blitz was a major trauma. It has been estimated that in the heaviest bombed towns and cities of the United Kingdom, up to 60 per cent of the total housing stock was damaged, and with it, the contents built up over a lifetime of saving. Salvaging belongings from the ruins was a sad task; many contemporary photographs show people picking through the wrecks of their houses in order to remove clocks, armchairs and empty budgie cages. Worse, if left too long, bombsites became rich pickings for those less scrupulous than others. Removal of items from people's bombed homes was looting – technically punishable by death in extreme cases – however, casual stealing of items was commonplace. Salvage squads were to be established later in the war, enabling what remained to be removed to safety – important when it was difficult to replace domestic items. Ultimately a 'utility furniture' scheme would operate, providing good quality, no frills essentials to those bombed out of their homes.

With the War Damage Act of 1941 it was compulsory for householders to pay for air raid insurance provided by the Government; under the 'Private Chattels Scheme' it was up to

Lapel badge worn by Rest Centre Staff.

'Salvaging' foodstuffs from a bombed grocer's shop on 20 March 1941; many people would have their possessions looted in this way. The Anderson shelter has done its job, however. (IWM HU 58554)

householders to decide whether they wanted to risk it or pay more. Other insurance schemes would promise little.

For most people, attacks such as these seemed personal; Hitler was lampooned, yet, as Mass Observation was to record, very few were to demand retaliation in the immediate aftermath of their ordeal. Glasgow schoolboy John Young observed the attack on his city:

I remember hearing the sirens and my mother lifting me out of bed upstairs in our semi-detached house, in the dark. We had just reached the living room when the bombs started falling. There was no time to go to our air raid Anderson shelter at the bottom of the garden and so we took shelter under our dining room table, luckily made of solid oak. There was an earsplitting explosion and the bricks of our chimney scattered into the room. All our windows were blown in and the roof ripped off.

The bed I was in only a few minutes earlier was shredded with glass. I was screaming at the time, and the next thing I knew was my father breaking into our house to rescue us.

One of several 'Blitz insurance' schemes, paid with single premiums, weekly. This offered little recompense.

Such stories are typical of the individual family ordeals, which together add up to the Blitz experience of a nation; they were repeated up and down the country during 1940–1.

After London, the bombing of Britain's cities took on a new form, as Luftflotte 3 commander Hugo Sperrle experimented with new ways of taking the war to his enemies, with new tactics to deliver the Nazi bombing strategy. The frequency of London's raids stuttered, and in their place came concerted attacks on Britain's smaller industrial cities. Though often short in duration, the ferocity of these attacks was to lay waste to many historic town centres, in many cases over hours. Coventry would be the first to experience this new form of attack.

'COVENTRATION'

Coventry was destined to be a prime target for the Luftwaffe, since it was home to many aircraft parts manufacturers (including Rolls-Royce, Hawker Siddeley and Vickers-Armstrongs), motor vehicle manufacturers such as Daimler and a host of other engineering works dedicated to the British war effort. This concentration of factories had not gone un-noticed by the German high command – and its potential as a target was uppermost in the minds of most residents. A surprising fact was the low rate of evacuation – only 3,000 children of 15,000 eligible left the city on the outbreak of war, and many of these were to return before the first bombs fell.

Coventry in 1940 still proudly displayed its medieval heritage, with narrow streets and a mix of building stock. Perhaps unusually, even for then, the city's industry was mixed in with its dwellings, stretching into its heart, preserving the green space of Warwickshire beyond the city boundaries. This mix was to be fatal when the bombers turned their attentions on the city.

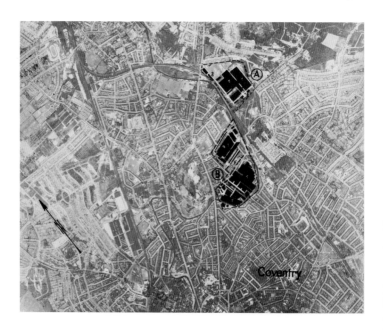

German pre-war aerial reconnaissance photograph of Coventry, showing both the Morris motor works (A) and the Rover aero engine works (B). (IWM C 5514)

The first bombs fell on the outskirts of Coventry in June 1940; by August, the city centre was receiving regular, if relatively light raids – some with incongruous results. The loss of the Rex cinema to a single bomb was widely commented upon – especially as it was due to show the epic *Gone With the Wind*. With the August raids came the arrival of the phenomenon known as 'trekking'. Nightly, people from all walks of life would leave the city for the surrounding countryside. At one end of the spectrum, wealthier Coventrians would drive and take one of the many properties advertised by enterprising citizens in nearby towns and villages; at the other, people would walk or take public transport, sleeping out under the stars. The fields and hedges of Warwickshire would be their refuge. The official view of this nightly exodus was disapproving; could this be evidence of the morale of the city starting to crack? Despite this concern, the trekkers were to return to the war effort by day; though they were nocturnal refugees (like those who flocked to the underground stations in London), there was no sense of abandonment of the city.

On 8 November, Coventry's fate was sealed. With the Blitz on London in progress, the RAF was instructed to bomb Munich – the symbolic capital of National Socialism – on the anniversary of the Beer Hall Putsch of 1923. Though little more than a demonstration, this attack at the party's roots was too much for the Nazis to bear, and an all-out attack on this small city in the heart of the Midlands was set – 'Operation *Mondscheinsonate*' (Moonlight Sonata) was to destroy Coventry's factories and industrial infrastructure, and strike terror into the population.

At 7.10 on the evening of 14 November, the sirens were sounded, heralding the arrival of the bombers from Luftflotte 3 – 515 bombers would attack the city in all. The 'air raid yellow' signal had been received three minutes earlier; within seconds the He 111 pathfinders of Kampfgruppe 100, directed by *X-Verfahren*, were dropping incendiaries on the heart of the city, lighting the way for the follow-up Ju 88 bombers. Edgar French recalls the opening minutes of the raid:

> About 7.15 or 7.30 p.m. we heard the thrum thrum of the German bombers and soon a continuous swishing sound. With that we went upstairs. On looking from the back bedroom window we could see a bluish white light like a curtain … The city was ringed by incendiaries, a prime marker for what was to follow. As we watched, the white light changed in patches to yellow orange and red. The fires had started.

Coventry was targeted for the first time with a mass of incendiaries and high-explosive SC bombs. The follow-up waves dropped a combination of high explosive and incendiaries. The high-explosive bombs rained into the medieval city centre, knocking out the utilities (the water supply, electricity network and gas mains) and cratering the roads; fighting to get through to the now-burning heart the fire service found its water supplies were running dry. Among the first buildings to succumb was the modern department store Owen Owen; the gothic Cathedral, a historic symbol to all who lived in the city, was to follow, set alight at around eight. Volunteer fire crews battled the flames against the odds, but with new fires springing up within the cathedral precinct, and in almost every narrow street surrounding, the cathedral was doomed, and with the water supplies interrupted, the centre of the city was to burn unchecked, the first of many firestorms of the war.

The raid reached its height at just before midnight, but the bomber waves continued to drop their loads every hour until the early morning; the 'raiders past' signal was received at 6.16 a.m., the all-clear sirens sounding. In that one night, more than 8,000 homes in Coventry were destroyed or seriously damaged (with more than 41,000 affected), along with around three quarters of the city's factories. Though nearly 450 enemy bombers had appeared over the city, only one was lost to the British defences; 30,000 incendiary bombs clustered in 880 'Molotov breadbaskets', over 1,500 tons of high explosives, and many large oil bombs intended to spread the fire were poured into the packed city centre. There was barely an undamaged building left in the city centre. Two hospitals, two churches and a police station were also among the damaged buildings. Approximately 600 people were killed (the precise death

Coventry after the raids: the shell of the destroyed gothic cathedral.

toll has never been established) and more than 1,000 were injured, over 850 of them seriously. The population of Coventry at the time was over 200,000; at least a quarter of these, probably many more, had trekked from the city that night. What might have happened if they had stayed?

Coventry schoolboy Jason Strike remembers the aftermath:

> It was just unbelievable. The stench of still smoking debris with firemen still damping down. Everywhere there was the sight and sound of once familiar buildings, being demolished because they were a safety hazard. There in the centre of the City stood the large burnt out shell of Owen and Owen; which if memory serves me right, was the biggest store in Coventry. The next horror to come was the nearby Cathedral, just another smouldering shell. The images are still vivid in my mind to this day.

The mass grave and monument to the dead of the air raids of 14/15 November 1940, London Road, Coventry.

The victims of the raid were to be buried together in a mass grave in London Road cemetery on 20 November. Private burials were prohibited for those who lived in the city; an unprecedented decision. But then, no other city had suffered like Coventry. The Germans coined a new verb for the destruction: *Coventrieren* – to 'Coventrate'.

THE PORTS

Britain's ports were her lifelines. Dependent on a large percentage of her food to be imported during pre-war days (70 per cent of its sugar, 80 per cent of its fruit, 90 per cent of its cereals and even 50 per cent of its meat), there had had to be a major shift in eating habits when rationing was first introduced. No longer could the nation afford to be profligate with such valuable resources, particularly when the Kriegsmarine was fighting an all-out war against the merchantmen that crossed the Atlantic loaded with supplies essential to the British war effort. The south coast ports had received the attention of the Luftwaffe from the earliest part of the war; with Göring tiring of attempting to grind down the capital, they were targeted again in November 1940. Portsmouth and its neighbour Southampton had been attacked regularly from the beginning; Southampton was to receive its heaviest attack on 30 November 1940, Portsmouth on 10 January 1941. Both would come close to being 'Coventrated'.

Southampton received its baptism of fire on 17 November, with a daylight raid, and then, barely ten days after Coventry had endured its worst night, its

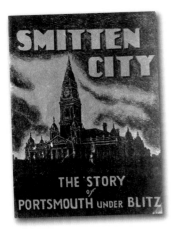

Smitten City: The Story of Portsmouth under Blitz. This was typical of many 'red sky' books, depicting cities in flames, produced after the war.

centre was targeted with incendiaries and high explosives, as eighty bombers attacked the city. Home to major docks, as well as significant factories – including that manufacturing the Supermarine Spitfire – the city was always going to be a target. And perhaps for this reason, and mirroring the nightly activity in Coventry, the surrounding countryside of Southampton would provide the safe haven people required to escape from the violence of the raids; 'trekking' was widespread, the nightly movement of a proportion of the city population away from its centre. Southampton's worst ordeal came over the weekend of 29–30 November. Here, following the pattern set at Coventry, over the Saturday and Sunday nights there were successive waves of bombers. The German pathfinders dropped incendiaries; the follow-up bombers, high-explosive SC bombs. For six hours or so each night, 120 aircraft poured their bombs into the centre of Southampton. Churches, shops and factories were all damaged; and while fire-fighters were drafted in from 75 districts damage to the infrastructure meant that, just like Coventry, the water supply was to dry up, preventing their work from taking hold.

The devastation was shattering, as Lellis Beale remembers:

> The centre of Southampton was almost completely destroyed. I remember walking along Above Bar which was the main shopping street. Where the shops had been hasty wooden fences had been put up to stop unwary people falling into the shops' basements, now visible.

And with the heat of the fires came controversy: had the city council, the mayor himself, abandoned the people to their fate, leaving with the 'trekkers'? There was the sense that the council was overwhelmed by the scale of the bombing. As with Coventry a fortnight before, though many had quit the city for good, others returned to their stricken city unbeaten, but resigned. The city was the smallest of the ports to be heavily blitzed at this period; yet it received over 700 tons of high explosives and thousands of incendiaries – with a loss of life that exceeded 630, with a further 898 seriously wounded.

With the Battle of the Atlantic raging, in February, Admiral Dönitz, commanding the Kriegsmarine, put the case for a renewed attack on British ports, and as such Hitler ordered the Luftwaffe to concentrate its efforts on these strategically important targets for the German war effort. Portsmouth, Plymouth, Bristol, Swansea, Merseyside, Tyneside, Clydebank, Belfast – all were selected for special attention, intended to both continue the attempt to break down civilian morale, and to destroy the industrial and military capabilities of these important centres of Britain's industrial and commercial might.

Plymouth would have its turn as one of the most blitzed cities in the spring of 1941, with the familiar pattern of over 1,000 SC high-explosive bombs, many parachute mines, thousands of incendiaries and 600 dead. Derek Dawes's memories are typical of many from this time, as Hitler tried to grasp back the advantage:

> During the course of the bombing I saw a lot of the city of Plymouth destroyed forever. It was a sight you could not really take in, to see local streets with houses on fire at night. The sky would seem to be full of bright red sparks and the smell of the smoke was very special, nothing else has ever smelt like it. The water supply ran out because so many water pipes had been bombed.

Plymouth's centre was devastated over two nights in March and five in April, 1941.

The pendulum would swing from one target to the next; the erratic nature of the German targeting appeared random, making it difficult to plan for the Nazis' next move. As with Coventry and Southampton, many local people were only too aware of the threat posed to their home city, as Helen Carter remembers:

> Liverpool and Birkenhead became Prime Targets, because of the geographical situation with America, who, although not in the war, were providing us with food and ammunition. It was at this time that Churchill had said to the Americans 'Give us the tools and we will finish the job', and of course there were a terrific number of ships being built at Cammell Laird's in Birkenhead. The men there were working full out.

Barrage Balloons on the Mersey, a painting by a fourteen-year-old schoolboy showing part of the Mersey defences.

35

Birkenhead and Liverpool on the Mersey would see the largest number of raids outside London, with massed attacks in late November, three nights in December, two in March and what became known as the May Blitz – seven sustained nights of violence by 800 massed bombers were meted out on Liverpool, Bootle and Birkenhead. As an extra defensive measure, Operation *Starfish* was enacted – the use of decoys. Here, offshore from the Wirral Peninsula, a small group of islands had buildings that were set alight electrically – these would draw the bombers away from their target, the bomb-aimers imagining that they were adding to the burning docks, while in fact they fell harmlessly into the sea. Similar decoys were to be used in other locations, such as Portsmouth. In Merseyside, the bombing was so severe – second only to the tonnage received by London – that rumours were started that 'martial law' had been declared; they were baseless. Some 4,000 people were killed in these raids.

After the raid: troops clearing up after a raid on the port town of Birkenhead, 15 March 1941. (IWM H 8138)

THE FIRESTORMS

With the raids on the ports in full swing, concentration on other urban and industrial centres was limited. London was having a respite from its ordeal; Coventry's destruction had been short and violent. The devastation visited upon Britain's significant but small industrial towns and ports had been

extensive. As well as that of Coventry, the centres of Portsmouth, Southampton and Plymouth had now more in common with the ruins of the Belgian city of Ypres after the First World War than the neat municipal boroughs they had once been. The ARP and fire services had suffered under the onslaught, and hard lessons had to be learned – particularly in the rescue of people from bombed buildings, as well as in the provision of water for the ever-thirsty fire appliances, since water mains were all too often shattered by high explosives. Morale held, but only after a shock-induced depression had briefly set in following the destruction of much-loved landmarks and historic centres. So far, the German bombing strategy had been erratic, but a pattern had emerged of pathfinders of Kampfgruppe 100 lighting the target, followed by high explosives dropped by the bombers of Luftflotte 3. This was all to change in December.

Our Blitz, the story of the Manchester firestorms.

Manchester was a major city of almost three-quarters of a million people; a transport centre and an important industrial and commercial hub, with the Manchester Ship Canal and other important transport links. The city had escaped with the usual isolated raids until late December, when on two nights following a Christmas break, the City was hit hard, and with a new tactic.

Liverpool and Birkenhead had already been hit in the run-up to Christmas, and with the fires from these raids still visible to the attackers, the Luftwaffe turned its attention to Manchester, on 21–22 December. The pathfinders of Kampfgruppe 100 lit the way. Follow-up bombers of Luftflotten 2 and 3 targeted the city with over 37,000 incendiary and 272 high-explosive bombs intended to wreak havoc in the city centre – and burn it to the ground. The plan nearly succeeded; the central Piccadilly area was a raging inferno.

The all-clear was to sound at 6.30 a.m., almost exactly twelve hours after the first warning. The bombers of Luftflotte 3 were to return the next evening, pouring more incendiaries into the city. Over 1,300 fires were started, with large areas of Manchester, Salford and Stretford devastated, leaving an estimated 684 people dead and 2,364 wounded.

This act was the prelude to one of the greatest raids made on London, on the night of 29–30 December 1940, when the Luftwaffe pounded the City with 100,000 separate incendiary bombs. Exceptionally well planned, the German attack had but one object – to set fire to the hub of the Empire, striking terror into the capital. Masterminded by Generalfeldmarschall Sperrle, the date was picked for two specific reasons: that the commercial

Manchester
blitzed; buildings
burn in the city,
December 1940.
(IWM H 6325)

A 1kg 'electron'
magnesium-bodied
and thermite-
cored incendiary
bomb. Hundreds of
thousands of these
were dropped
over Britain during
the war. This one
was kept as a
souvenir by a
London fireman.

centre of the city would likely be deserted in the run-up to the New Year holiday, so that there would be few people to attack the incendiaries; and, that the River Thames, guaranteed to supply extra water to the hard pressed fire crews, would be at an exceptionally low state of tide, a slim ribbon in its normally wide channel. Most of the city offices would be empty and locked; there would be few 'fire watchers' to deal with the 'electron' bombs that would be poured into the centre of the city. Fortunately, those on duty at St Paul's Cathedral, its dome a great symbol of the capital, would not be found wanting when called upon to act.

Once again the fire starters of the elite pathfinder Kampfgruppe 100 led the attack, their target picked out by their onboard *X-Gerat*. Unloading their incendiaries, this was the first time that London had been attacked with so many of the fire-dealing bombs. There were simply too many (and too few people) to attack them. In the early winter-dark sky, the streets and buildings of the city began to burn, and the follow-up waves of bombers from Kampfgeschwader 51 released their loads of 'Molotov breadbaskets' directly down the throats of the flames, and into an area that had know fire intimately before, during the Great Fire of London in 1666. The City streets from the Guildhall to St Paul's Cathedral, from Moorgate to Aldersgate, and Old Street to Cannon Street (packed as they were with architectural jewels) would be the centre of the bombers' attentions. Just as in 1666, the fires would soon spread out of control, and develop into major conflagrations. In the thick of it, tackling the fires head-on, even the stalwart firemen of the London Fire Brigade and their Auxiliary colleagues would soon be overwhelmed. There would never be enough water to deal with the job in hand. Gladys Stiles was witness to the scene:

> One night a few days after Christmas the bombers first dropped incendiary bombs, they came down nonstop, plopping like hail stones. My father and his team [of fire watchers] climbed onto the roofs and kicked as many as they could down into the street. Many fires were started that night and we thought of it ever after as the second great fire of London. No explosive bombs were dropped but there were explosions of appliances in the buildings, we thought at one stage some of the buildings were being blown up to stop the fires, as once again water had run out.

Critically, Sir Christopher Wren's great baroque masterpiece, St Paul's, would come under attack as fires raged all around Paternoster Square. Nervously, the Cathedral Fire Watch worked tirelessly to deal with white-hot burning magnesium of those bombs that fell into the precinct; when one penetrated the lead-covered dome, and plumes of smoke arose from the

Herbert Mason's classic image of St Paul's Cathedral rising from within the flames, during the night of 29 December 1940. (IWM HU 36220)

This ash tray is made from stone and lead from the blitz-damaged Houses of Parliament, 1941.

Cathedral, everyone feared the worst. The radio broadcaster Edward Morrow reported what he saw to the American people: the loss of the great building. But his report was premature – the incendiary dropped harmlessly through the dome down to the tiles below, where it could be dealt with by the Blitz-seasoned Cathedral Watch. The Cathedral would be saved, while all around burned. Herbert Mason of the *Daily Mail* was on hand to take one of the most famous pictures of the Second World War, an image of deliverance – the shining dome rising ethereally above the fires of the City, some 1,500 separate major incidents. The Guildhall itself, eight of Wren's other churches – themselves built after the Great Fire of 1666 – Paternoster Row and The Old Bailey would all be savagely destroyed. But the city survived its 'Second Great Fire', and lessons were learned.

The final phase of the Luftwaffe's main bombing campaign was to come in the spring of 1941, ports and arms towns across the United Kingdom taking the brunt of the destruction. The Liverpool eight-day 'May Blitz' was particularly protracted, but many other cities 'copped it' including Belfast, Clydeside, Bristol, Cardiff and Swansea, and Hull. The last major attack on London was on 10 May: 515 bombers destroyed or damaged many important buildings in Westminster, including the seat of Parliament, and such fashionable addresses as Carlton House Terrace and Pall Mall; 1,634 people were killed and a similar number wounded. The last raid of the Blitz proper was over Birmingham, on 16 May; like many others, this city, noted for its arms factories, had suffered regularly since August 1940, and was the third most blitzed centre in Britain after London and Merseyside. It was to suffer to the end.

THE RESPONSE

With Britain's anti-aircraft provision found wanting, there was a pressing need for new weapons and equipment to tackle the raiders: radar, both to help aim the AA guns and to direct the new purpose-built night fighter capability of the fast, strong and powerfully equipped Bristol Beaufighter. With the use of radar in both cases came successes unheard of in 1940; from the start of 1941 the toll on the Luftwaffe started to build, with monthly losses increasing dramatically (28 in January, 124 in May).

After the fire raids of 1940, and the blitzes of 1941, distinct changes were also made to Britain's civil defence. Though the ARP services had been severely tested, the system had proved its worth, and from 1941, it was given a new identity as 'Civil Defence'. More pressing was the need to shake up the fire services, which had a miscellany of regional structures, training standards and even equipment. Deploying brigades in support of each other had been a major headache, and this had contributed to the problems experienced in Manchester and London in late 1940.

The structure of the pre-war fire service owed much to its Victorian origins, and consisted of a large number of separate brigades, each with their own methods of working and equipment and each under the control of the local fire authority. In the provinces, this approach was reasonable, but in Greater London, the hub and junction of several counties, there were around sixty-seven individual brigades, with much potential for confusion and duplication of effort. The need for a single, unified fire service using the same regulations and, where possible, equipment, was born from the great incendiary-fuelled fires of late 1940. And so, in August 1941, the centrally-controlled National Fire Service (NFS) was created, amalgamating the local brigade structure, and incorporating the volunteer AFS force on a full-time basis. At its height, the NFS was to have 350,000 members. Such a coordinated response was developed to ensure that 'Britain would not burn'; the NFS would be deployed in number during the later attacks on Britain.

The 'Second Great Fire of London' had also alerted the authorities to the inadequacies of the system of fire control. Individually, the magnesium incendiary bombs dropped during the Blitz and beyond could be controlled by sand or stirrup pump – as long as it could be reached in good time. Wartime fires were exacerbated by the fact that by the time the fire services attended, it was too late, as the hot-burning magnesium of the 'electron' incendiary had burnt its way through the roofs of helpless buildings. Up to 1941, wardens did not even have the right of entry granted to fire authorities, so British factories and domestic premises, often tightly locked, were left unprotected.

To combat this, an unpaid force of fire watchers, armed with helmet and stirrup pump, were mobilised, and every industrial premises had an organised rota – although many resented the extra burden placed upon them after a hard day's work – with a minimum requirement to carry out 48 hours' duty in any four-week period. These men and women were trained to locate and deal with incendiaries before they had taken hold of a building, before calling in the NFS. In August 1941, a new organisation, the Fire Guard, would take over fire-watching. Like the NFS, the Fire Guard grew in stature in 1942, when it was to be tested during the 'Baedeker' raids, engaged in saving the historic structure of Britain's ancient towns and cities from destruction.

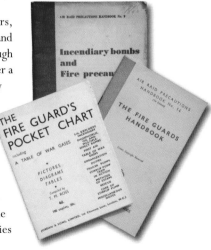

National Fire Service (NFS) cap badges. The NFS was raised in response to the fire raids in Britain in late 1940.

The Fire Guard was established to help combat fires before they got out of control; this is some of the guide literature available.

REVENGE

TO ALL INTENTS and purposes, the intensive blitz was over by the mid part of 1941. However, following British mass aerial raids on Germany, reprisals were ordered by Hitler in April 1942 – the attacks on the centres of the historic cities of Exeter, Bath, Norwich, Canterbury and York among others – raids which severely tested the Civil Defence Services for two months during these 'Baedeker' raids. Although full air raids became rare after 1942, they were still prevalent, with 'tip-and-run' raids being common on Britain's coastal towns. In these attacks, fast fighter-bombers (Focke-Wulf Fw 190 or Messerschmitt Bf 110) arrived without warning, and delivered their bombs, often accompanied by machine-gunning of the streets. And for the 'front line' city of Dover, there was the added threat of long-range shelling, an ever-present threat until Canadian troops captured the guns at Cap Gris Nez – at which point they sent the mayor a telegram.

There was to be a last gasp attempt at bombing Britain conventionally, when Göring ordered the Luftwaffe to resume attacks in November 1943. Severely depleted from its exertions in the East, and under increasing pressure from Allied air attacks in the West, the 500 or so aircraft mustered were of widely varying types. The last conventional air raids on the capital – known as the 'Little' or 'Baby Blitz' – in January to March 1944 – were disastrous for the Luftwaffe: over 300 of the 500 aircraft were lost.

The final air assault on Britain was the launching of the 'V' weapons offensive following the Allied invasion of Europe in June 1944. First the pilotless 'flying bomb', the V-1, nicknamed the 'buzz bomb' or 'doodlebug' wrought havoc over London with over 6,000 people killed and 16,000 wounded; just as the AA defences were deployed with some success, the deadly V-2 rocket made its presence felt – killing nearly 3,000 people, with twice that number seriously injured.

THE BAEDEKER BLITZ

The Baedeker raids were pure retaliation; revenge raids (*Vergeltungsangriffe*) by the Luftwaffe for the bombing of the ancient Hanseatic town of Lübeck

Opposite:
Bomb damage to
a London street,
c. 1945.

The *Baedeker Guide to Great Britain*, 1937. This would be the source of inspiration for the 'Baedeker Blitz'.

by the RAF on 28–9 March 1942. Lübeck burned; Arthur 'Bomber' Harris was intent on destroying a moderately important industrial town, rather than failing to achieve anything against a heavily defended city. Lübeck, with its many timber-framed medieval buildings, was chosen as it was likely to burn when hit by a large proportion of incendiaries – the technique had been perfected by the Luftwaffe itself against Coventry.

Photograph showing the damage to St Augustine's Abbey and its surroundings following the Baedeker raids on Canterbury, May–June 1942. (IWM Q(HS) 299)

In retaliation for the Lübeck raid the Germans bombed Exeter on 23 April 1942 – it was to be ineffectual, but the bombers would return. This was the first of the 'Baedeker' raids – so-called after the famous German Baedeker travel guides, the cities to be attacked singled out for their historic importance alone, based on the number of stars awarded by the guide to the site. Three stars was the minimum requirement; historic centres and buildings would be deliberately targeted. Some, like Bath, had no defences.

The Baedeker raids were conducted in two periods between April and June 1942, with Exeter (23 and 24 April, 3 May), Bath (25 and 26 April), Norwich (27 and 29 April) and York (28 April) bombed in the first phase; Canterbury followed in the second (31 May, 2 and 6 June). One-third of the city area was laid waste. Across all the raids on these five cities a total of 1,637 civilians were killed and 1,760 injured, and over 50,000 houses were destroyed, with many notable buildings lost or wrecked, the cathedrals of Norwich, Exeter, the church of St George's in Canterbury, and York's medieval Guild Hall included. In Bath alone, 19,000 buildings were destroyed, though the Royal Crescent was to survive. Roy Scott remembers the bombing of Norwich:

> The bombing and the drone of the planes finally ceased and some long time after, the single note of the air raid siren signalled the end of the raid. My mother did not lead us out from our hideaway straight away, not because she was afraid of the return of the German bombers, I think it was because she was afraid of what she would find if we came out.

PURE REVENGE

The first of Hitler's revenge weapons, the Vergeltungswaffe 1 or 'V-1', designed to take the fight back to the British in a particularly brutal and random manner, were prepared in the Autumn of 1943. Consisting of a simple, winged fuselage of welded steel, and packed with 850 kg of Amatol explosive, the weapon was simply designed to bring terror to the shores of

Cut-away diagram of the Vergeltungswaffe 1 (V-1), from a publication in aid of the Fire Services Benevolent Fund, 1944.

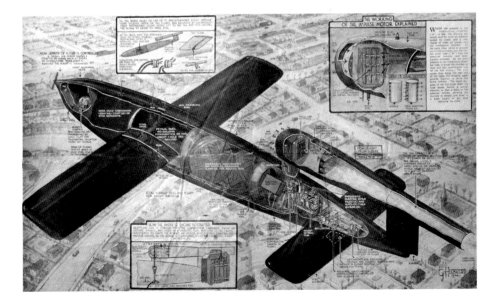

Blue plaque
marking the site
of impact of the
first V-1 to land in
Britain, in Grove
Road, Mile End,
London.

Victims of a flying
bomb incident at
St John's Hill,
Clapham, on
13 June 1944.
(IWM HU 91464)

the British Isles. The V-1 was distinguished by the throbbing sound of its pulsejet, a sound that would cut out as the aircraft's fuel became depleted, the engine spluttering before cutting out and the bomb turning headlong for earth, with an eerie hush before impact. These sounds would lead to the weapon being christened with the friendly names 'buzz-bomb', or 'doodle-bug'. There was nothing friendly about the actual bomb itself. As Londoner Victor Spink remembered:

If the deafening pulse engine cut out on the approach there was a heart stopping 7 to 12 second silence. This terrible silence was followed by a huge bang as it exploded just before it hit the ground or on rooftops. Lucky folk like us not too close to the blast just had their windows blown in and ornaments knocked off their mantelpiece. We kept our window curtains closed even on the hottest of summer days, which prevented glass from the windows flying into our rooms. If the tone of the droning engine changed as it passed overhead, then my mother would say to us, 'its all right dears, it's going now'. Even today if I hear just a recording of a Doodlebug I instinctively go into a flight mode and want to move away from the windows.

The flight of a V-1 could be watched, the horror of its stall and its steep dive obvious to all.

Launched from a simple 'ski-ramp', sites were constructed along the French, and later Dutch coast, and by June 1944 – just as the Allies were landing in Normandy – they were ready for action. London was to receive the first of these unmanned, pulse-jet propelled aircraft on 13 June 1944, when ten were launched. Only four would reach England, the first landing harmlessly near Swanscombe in Kent. Near Mile End in London's East End, however, a bridge was destroyed and six people killed and nine injured. A plaque records this event today on the rebuilt bridge at Grove Road. The V-1 was very simply aimed, and set roughly on target by gyroscopes; that target was permanently set on Tower Bridge.

The V-1 attacks became sustained, typically a hundred a day were launched, with 500 over the first weekend of deployment (16–17 June 1944). The majority of the bombs fell on the southern and eastern parts of the city. South of London, Croydon was on the flight path, and suffered severely, taking 142 hits. A large number were to fall across Kent, and many others overshot into Essex, several hitting Winston Churchill's Parliamentary constituency in Wanstead and Woodford. The single most devastating bomb attack fell on 17 June; here, close by the Cabinet's secret war rooms, the Guards Chapel was hit during a service; 121 people were killed, and 60 badly injured. There were many tragedies enacted by this weapon. In all, a total of 9,251 V-1s were launched at Britain, the vast majority aimed at London; 2,515 would reach the city, killing 6,184 civilians and injuring 17,981.

Site of the first V-2 to land in Britain, at Staveley Road, Chiswick.

The air defences had a new threat to respond to: barrage balloons were laid in their flight path, AA guns trained on their distinctive shapes, even fighter aircraft deployed to tip them over. A more potent threat, however, was the supersonic rocket attacks by the next generation revenge weapon, the V-2. Launched from The Hague in the Netherlands, the first was fired on 8 September – it took just 5 minutes to reach the capital, landing at Staveley Road, Chiswick. It hit the street at 6.44 p.m., gouging a crater 30 feet across and 8 feet deep. The blast killed three people, injured 22 and demolished six houses, announcing a new terror for the capital, a terror campaign that was to last to the end of the war (V-1s also continued to be launched).

The rocket's most devastating strike was on 25 November 1944 at the Woolworth's store in New Cross Gate. Woolworth's had been especially popular that day: people were queueing for aluminium saucepans,

a rare commodity when this war material was needed for Spitfires. Travelling at twice the speed of sound, the rocket destroyed the store completely, leaving a huge hole where it had previously stood, killing 168 people and seriously injuring 121.

Barbara Smith was a young teenager when the Woolworth's V-2 fell:

> As I hurried home I saw many people who were injured, and others were dead and lying on the pavements and in the road. Ambulances and fire engines were parked nearby, attending to the injured and dying. The air was filled with grit and dust. There was a huge crater on the Woolworth site where the V-2 had fallen. I had been at the Woolworths store visiting every Saturday morning with a friend, but that particular Saturday, I'm glad to say that I hadn't gone.

Bob Davis was eighteen at the time of the attack. He writes:

> It was November 25th, 1944, 11.55 a.m. [The bus] got to New Cross Gate Station; I got up from my seat in preparation to get off at the next stop. A V-2 Rocket hit a Woolworth store no more than fifty yards from the bus. I was thrown up the aisle of the bus between the seats smashing my head against a seat leg. I soon became conscious and the debris was still coming down and it was pitch black. All the windows on the bus were gone – the stairs, what was left of them, I was able to slide down. When I got to the bottom, I saw the bus tickets covering the back deck. There was no sign of the conductor nor were there any signs of any of the passengers from either upstairs or downstairs. I later learned that the bus has been 'spun like a top' and that the paint had all been stripped off the outside of the bus by the intense blast.

A modern reconstruction of the much-feared V-2 rocket, and a commemorative plaque at New Cross Gate showing what one rocket could do.

LONDON BOROUGH OF LEWISHAM

In memory of the 168 people who died and those injured in the V2 rocket attack that landed here 25th November 1944

As there was no practical way of stopping these rockets in flight, the only way to stop them was by bombing the launch sites – this was largely ineffectual – or capturing them on the ground. This was only achieved at the end of March, after the Allies had managed to cross the Rhine and advance deep into the Netherlands, and sustained bombardment continued until then. The very last missiles arrived on 27 March 1945, with one of them killing 134 people and injuring 49 when it hit a block of flats in Stepney. Altogether, 1,115 V-2s were fired at London, killing 2,754 people and injuring 6,523 others, a terrifying chapter in the history of the 'London Blitz'.

Left: Post-war replacement for the building destroyed at New Cross Gate. The plaque on page 48 can be seen on the wall to the left of the Iceland store.

Below: Photograph depicting the site of a V-2 rocket attack in East London, in which nine people were killed and fifteen seriously injured. The cleared site shows the extent of the devastation. (IWM CH 152380)

AFTERMATH

THE BLITZ on Britain's cities in 1940–1, the Baedeker raids of 1942, tip-and-run raids and the V-weapons offensives had left an indelible mark on the country. Enduring everything that Hitler could throw at the country has now become almost a shorthand for British pluck and determination, such that in times of adversity it is common to remember those dark days when Hitler tried unsuccessfully to crush the spirit of a people. Despite the imposition of the blackout and rationing, the mood of the nation – variously described by historians of differing views as the 'spirit of the Blitz' or the 'myth of the Blitz' – was a positive one, based on shared suffering and forbearance. And among the many slogans produced by the war, 'Britain can take it' was an ultimate sign of this defiance. Yet left behind was a trail of devastation that spread across the country.

The reconstruction of the blitzed cities of Britain was destined to take some time, and would, in many cases, reshape in earnest the layout and atmosphere of once-ancient centres for ever, remodelled on modernist principles. Planning for a new start commenced in earnest in 1943; there was to be no repeat of the empty promises of 'a land fit for heroes' made to the previous post-war generation; this time there would be new houses, new towns and new spaces for recreation.

Provision of housing for those who had been bombed out was the first priority; prefabricated buildings – prefabs – were designed and built in Britain from such materials as asbestos concrete panels, and were announced to the world by Winston Churchill in March 1944. Over 156,000 would be built, often on the edges of towns and cities; one estate of 156 in Catford, South London – the Excalibur Estate – continues to fight off the demands of planners for their demolition today.

To build the new Britain, post-war Acts of Parliament enshrined integrated planning principles; new open spaces and the protection of Britain's countryside were the key components, becoming law in 1947 and determining the development of Britain for much of the remainder of the twentieth century. The brave new world would be well designed and fit for purpose.

Opposite:
Photo of St Paul's Cathedral in 1944, showing the extensive bomb damage surrounding it.
(IWM GSA 557)

A bell made from the aluminium derived from crashed German aircraft, and sold in aid of the RAF Benevolent Fund.

In 1940, during the Blitz, Lord Reith was appointed as Minister of Works and Buildings. Under his guidance, the bombed cities were advised to plan for the future 'boldly and comprehensively', without particular regard to who would pay. With town planning a new and burgeoning discipline, noted academic Professor Abercrombie of the University of London was called upon to help with the design of the new centres that would sweep away in bold terms the ancient, but now destroyed centres of many of Britain's cities.

In London, reconstruction was piecemeal, with Abercrombie's *Plan for London* (1943) and *Greater London Plan* (1944) recommending the relocation of some of the city's most blitzed populations – in the East End, for instance – in bright new purpose-built towns on the outer ring of the city, outside the new 'green belt'. But it was in small, sharply blitzed and devastated cities (such as Plymouth, Coventry and Southampton) that the Reith-inspired 'bold and comprehensive' plans would have the greatest impact. Professor Abercrombie was to be inspirational in the development of the *Plan for Plymouth* (1943); the man he replaced at the

The devastation of central Portsmouth, ready for development.

University of London, Professor S. D. Adshead, was to do the same for Southampton. In Coventry, City Architect Donald Gibson was its author.

All three cities envisaged remodelled and reconstructed city centres employing the best in modernist design. Plymouth was completely rebuilt, its ancient street layout discarded for a new design; objections and meddling by ministers and ministries altered the design to its detriment. In Southampton, Adshead's bold plans were watered down as the city lost faith. It is perhaps only Gibson's Coventry that remains as a bright, shining example of modernist design, with a shopping centre that does justice to the memory of those who lost their lives in the destruction of the city. Vibrant now, the architectural masterpiece of Coventry Cathedral reminds visitors of the terror that can still be delivered from the air to innocent civilians on the ground.

Many scars remain as evidence of the Blitz if one should care to look for them; a heavily blitz-damaged wall in Exhibition Road, South Kensington, is there to be seen by all who pass by.

The main layout of streets in Abercrombie's *Plan for Plymouth*, 1943.

An example of post-war modernism in Coventry, built in the wake of the city's devastation.

This blitz-damaged wall on Exhibition Road, South Kensington, London, has been preserved as a memorial.

FURTHER READING

'The Blitz' has received much attention by authors, and there are many locally produced accounts of the attacks on specific cities. The reading suggested here is just a small selection of what is available.

Anon. *Britain under Fire*. Country Life.
Anon. *The British People at War*. Odhams Press.
Anon. *Ourselves in Wartime*. Odhams Press.
Anon. *Fire Over London*. Hutchinson, 1941.
Anon. *Front Line 1940–1941*. HMSO, 1942.
Billingham, Mrs A. *Civil Defence in War*. John Murray & The Pilot Press, 1941.
Doyle, P. *ARP and Civil Defence in the Second World War*. Shire, 2010.
Evans, P. & Doyle, P. *The 1940s Home*. Shire, 2010.
Fitzgibbon, C. *The Blitz*. Wingate, 1957.
Gardiner, J. *Wartime Britain 1939–1945*. Headline, 2004.
Glover, C. W. *Civil Defence*. Chapman & Hall, 1938.
Gregg, J. *The Shelter of the Tubes: Tube Sheltering in Wartime London*. Capital Transport, 2001.
Harrisson, T. *Living through the Blitz*. Collins, 1976.
Johnson, D. *The City Ablaze: The Second Great Fire of London, 29th December, 1940*. William Kimber, 1980.
Longmate, N. *Air Raid*. Hutchinson, 1976.
Longmate, N. (Ed.) *The Home Front, An Anthology 1938–1945*. Chatto & Windus, 1981.
O'Brien, T. *Civil Defence*. HMSO & Longmans, Green & Co., 1955.
Pile, General Sir F. *Ack-Ack: Britain's Defence Against Air Attack in the Second World War*. George Harrap & Co., 1949.
Price, A. *Blitz on Britain, 1939–45*. History Press, 2009.
Wakefield, K. *The Blitz Then and Now*. Volumes 1–3, After the Battle, 1988.
Webb, E. & Duncan, J. *Blitz over Britain*. Spellmount, 1990.
Whiting, C. *Britain Under Fire: The Bombing of Britain's Cities, 1940–45*. Leo Cooper, 1999.
Ziegler, P. *London at War*. Sinclair Stevenson, 1995.

INDEX

Page numbers in italics refer to illustrations

Abercrombie, Professor Patrick 52
Abyssinia 7
Adshead, Professor S. D. 53
Air raids *4*
Air Raid Precautions (ARP) and Civil Defence (CD) 10–1, 15, 40–1
Air Raid Precautions Act 11
Air raid shelter *3*, 19, 22
Air raid sirens *12*, 19, 29
Air raid warnings 13
Air raid wardens 10–1
Anderson, Dr David 13
Anderson, Sir John 10
Anderson shelters *12, 13*, 13–4, *22*, 27, *29*,
Anti-Aircraft Command 9, 10
Anti-Aircraft guns (AA, Ack Ack) 7, *8*, 9, 22, 40, 47
Auxiliary Fire Service 11, 39, 41

Baedeker raids 5, 41, 43–5, 51
Baldwin, Stanley 7
Balloon Command 9
Barrage balloons 8, 9
Bath 43, 44, 45
Battle of Britain 15
Belfast 34
Berlin 19
Birmingham 40
Blackout *3*, 11, *12*, 12–3
Blitz 5, 17–23, 27–41, 51
'Blitz insurance' *29*
Blitzkrieg 5
Bombs and mines 25, 27, 31, 34, 35, 45–6
Bristol 34

Canterbury 43, *44*
Casualties 6, 7, 21, 23, 27, 33, 43, 44, 45, 47

Civil Defence (ARP) 8, 10–1
Chamberlain, Neville 7
Churchill Winston 47, 51
Clydebank 34
Croydon 47
'Coventration' 30, 33
Coventry *1*, 24, 27, 30–3, 34, 35, 52, *53*
Czechoslovakia 7

Dönitz, Admiral Karl 34
Douhet, Guilio 6
Dover 43
'Droppers' 15
Dunkirk 18

Epping Forest 22
Evacuation 11, 30
Exeter 43, 44

'Fire bomb Fritz' 25
Firebrace, Commander Sir Aylmer 21
Fire Guard 25, 41
Firestorms 36–40
Fire watchers 38, 41

Gibson, Donald 53
Göring, Reichsmarshall Hermann 19, 22, 43

Harrisson, Tom 5
Harris, Air Chief Marshall Arthur 44
Heinkel He 111 24, *25*
Hitler, Adolf 7, 22, 45

Incendiaries 25, 31, 35, 37, *38*, 41

Jones, Dr R.V. 24
Junkers 88 (Ju88) *16*, 24, *25*

Kampfgeschwader 24, 31, 38
Kampfgruppen 24, 37, 38
Kent 17, 47
Knickebein 24

'Little (Baby) Blitz' 43
London 15, 17, *18*, 19–23, 27, 36, 37–40, *43*, 47–9, 52

'London Barrage' 9, 23
London docks 19, 21
London Fire Brigade 39
London Underground ('tube') 15, *15*, 31
Lübeck 44
Luftflotten 23, 24, 29
Luftwaffe *16*, 21, 23–5

Manchester 24, *37–8*, 40
Mason, Herbert *39*, 40
Mass Observation 5, *6*, 15, 29
'May Blitz' (Merseyside) 36, 40
Merseyside (Liverpool, Birkenhead, Bootle) 34, *35, 36*, 37, 40
Ministry of Home Security 5, 27, *28*
'Molotov breadbaskets' 25, 34, 38
Mondscheinsonate, Operation (Moonlight Sonata) 31
Morrisson, Herbert 15
'Morrisson sandwich' 14
Morrison shelter 14
Morrow, Edward 40
Munich 31
Munich Agreement 7, 14

National Fire Service (NFS) 41
Norwich 43, 44

Observer Corps 8
Orkney 17

Pankhurst, Sylvia 7
'Passive defence' 10–1
Pile, General Frederick 9
Plymouth 34, 35, 52, *53*
Portsmouth 17, 33, *34*, 36, *52*
Prefabricated houses ('prefabs') 51
Private Chattels Scheme 29

Radar 8, 9, 40
Reconstruction 51–3
Reith, Lord John 52
Rest Centres 28
Royal Air Force 8, 19, 24

St Paul's Cathedral *39–40*, *50*
Sea Lion, Operation 19
Searchlights 7
'Second Great Fire of London' *26*, 37–40, 41
'September Blitz' (London) 22, 27
Shelling (of Dover) 43
Shrapnel collecting *9*, 10
Southampton 33, 34, 35, 52
Spanish Civil War 7
'Spirit of the Blitz' 5, 51
Sperrle, General Feldmarschall Hugo *24*, 29, 37
'Starfish', Operation 36
Steel-Bartholomew Committee 8
Surface shelters ('Morrisson Sandwich') *14*
Swansea 34

Thames Haven 19
'Trekking' 31, 34
Tyneside 34

V (*Vergeltungsangriffe*)-weapons offensive 6, 42–3, 45–9
V(*Vergeltungswaffe*)-1 ('doodlebug', 'buzzbomb') 45–7
V(*Vergeltungswaffe*)-2 42, 47–9

War damage 53, *54*
War Damage Act 28–9
Westminster 20, 22
Women's Auxiliary Air Force 9
Women's voluntary Service 28

X-*Verfahren* (*X-Gerät*) 24, 31, 38

York 43, 44
Ypres 37

Zeppelins 6